Count Their Lives
in Womanyears

For shared community
Barbara Funderburk

Count Their Lives in Womanyears

Barbara Funderburk

CHAPEL HILL
PRESS, INC.

Cover painting: The author's painting depicts generations of Southern women piecing together and helping unite their family farmlands.

ISBN 1-880849-49-6
Library of Congress Catalog: 2002109162

Printed in Korea

05 04 03 02 01 10 9 8 7 6 5 4 3 2 1

To my mother, Faire Lathan Funderburk,
for her constant love and
encouragement over the years

With special thanks to Mrs. Frances Vick
for her support and help in reviewing the manuscript

Foreword

A swift glance at the digital clock tells me I'm already running late. The numbers flip forward in determined cadence beyond any recognition of real time: just the brief flash of a minute to be erased by the ones to come. Last memo dictated, overnight work ready in the briefcase, desk cleared—all set.

Swirl into the dam break of traffic—computerize the movement in your head, watch for a break, grab your chance, move in quickly. Stream through concrete passes with snaking lines of steel and rubber and backwashes of people flowing past in arcs of color. People, cars, buildings—all in blurred lines of slashing, colored arrows as speed pushes us toward the vertex of lines pinpointed at the horizon . . . always the horizon. Flinging onto an artery off the main highway vein, the pulse begins to slow. The chase is nearly done.

Leaving the suburbs as postcards in the rearview mirror, time becomes elastic. The years roll back in rhythm with the miles logged on the odometer. Fifteen miles, fifteen years. Twenty miles, twenty years. Times spreads laterally now—across the fields, playing in light points off shimmering ponds, mellowing on the sides of old barns. This is where I come from. This place . . . this way . . . where time is felt, not counted. Here . . . where time is not in the negative-G, gut-pull towards a vertex on the horizon, but in the subtle meld of season into season with the gentle spiral of life in its folds.

And they are here, too. I feel them as I glide along the road. Those few now left who measure their lives in womanyears. A year is much more than a number to them. It is meant to measure the size of things in their own world. To these farm women, it's "the year the big storm came" or "the year the littlest'un was born" or "the year of the big crop" or "the year Pa died." Years known by what the good and bad of living brings. Time forged as another link in a chain of memories spanning generations. Womanyears.

There aren't many of these women left—the ones who were born and raised on a farm and have continued to live that life through all their years. They're mostly of my grandmother's generation, the early 20th century. Their daughters and granddaughters have, nearly all of us, moved away to the towns and cities to forge new worlds for ourselves. When her generation passes away—and it is quickly, and with a sigh, doing so—a way of life and time will have gone with them.

So why should I care? My life has always been lived in a world far-removed from theirs—a world existing physically close to them, yet galaxies apart with few innerspace visitors crossing either way. Their life holds nothing that I need. I buy my food at a grocery store; I have a car to take me where I wish to go; I have a doctor, a dentist, and a beautician on call. I have a college degree and a career. I have credit when money runs short. I have all the modern appliances: air-conditioning, heating. I have plenty of clothes. If life gets too dreary, I can even get an analyst to help rid me of my worries. I have available any form of entertainment I could care to indulge in.

So why should I care if their black wash pots sit empty? What could it matter if there were no more dresses made of chickenfeed sacks? So what, if I don't eat another grape pie with the seeds still in it? Why should it bother me if someone bought their butter churns at an auction to use as planters? What difference if the slop bucket for pigs eats itself up?

Perhaps it is precisely because of the differences in my life and theirs that I do care. The comforts and necessities of my life depend completely on someone else's supplying them to me. Even though I exchange money for them, they come from somewhere beyond me. Yet my grandmother's generation (such a short span between us!) eked out their needs from the land—and a few comforts along the way, too. There was no middleman for them to depend on. I view myself as independent, yet I do not create directly even one of the basics necessary to keep me alive, as they did.

But, of course, I could learn those basic skills, couldn't I? The skills, yes. But what about the rest of it? What about the sheer physical endurance, the tenacity and courage to keep going under continuing hardship, with nothing but faith and hope to put your heart in? What about the humility to accept it and the temerity to rise above it? Would

I be able to develop that sense of humor that twinkles in their eyes and ripples in their laughter? Were my hands to become as gnarled as theirs, would they still have that gentlest of touches? Could I find pleasure and joy in the simplest things in life as they did?

Yes, I care deeply about their black wash pots and their chicken feed sack dresses and their butter churns and their slop buckets. Those things represent courage, faith, and love to me. Count their lives in womanyears.

Miss Sally

A soft breeze was lazily slapping the sagging crib door against the gray-boned wall when a small burst of pastel came swirling around the corner. Springing up the stepping-stones to the crib in a whirlwind of feet and giggles, she triumphantly squealed, "Grandma! I beat you to the crib!" Grandma chuckled and acknowledged that remarkable feat as she set her empty basket on the raised floor and pulled herself, with some effort, up into the corncrib.

Each time, this forage in late ochre afternoons led them through weathered buildings full of untold mysteries and treasures. Up on high shelves, down in old feeding boxes, in the corners of empty stalls, through scattered hay in the lofts, in the henhouse proper and hen boxes perches on shed walls, there were always the brown-shelled treasures waiting in old nests and the thrill of new nests to find. And each time, the child met with something she hadn't seen or known about before. Life constantly unfolded before her whenever she and Grandma gathered up the eggs.

Along with the new, there were familiar things to revel in once more—the soft smell of cottonseed, the thin pallet crunch of barn straw underfoot, the coarse touch of gunnysacks stuffed with oats and wheat, the fluff of the newest litter of kittens, the lowing of cows coming in from the pasture.

This corncrib was a new place to look for eggs. Some of the old nests were going empty. Seeing hens coming out, Grandma suspected they must have taken up laying here. The crib seemed dark and empty as the two of them came in from the bright sun. Then, one by one, objects began to form out of the dark, and they launched a rummaging search for the suspected nests.

In a far, dark corner of the crib, a ray of light had slipped between two cracked ribs in the wall. It streamed, pencil-thin, through the deep velour shadows. Enchanted, the little girl moved closer to watch golden particles of dust dancing and swirling through the light beam. Her eyes followed the long, tumbling weave of golden light and dust across the raven-black space. She found it finally spilling onto a piece of faded pink calico lying wadded on the floor. Curious, she picked up the crumpled mass and turned to ask, "Grandma, what's this?"

The old woman gave the calico a shake and held it at arm's length for inspection. A look of surprise slipped over her face. She sat down heavily on a sack of corn and, laying the cloth across her lap, began gently to smooth the wrinkles from it.

In a voice full of wonder, she said, "Well, I sw'an! It's always been a puzzle to me as to what in the world ever happened to this thing. It belonged to your mama when she was a little girl. It's her cotton sack. I made it for her when she wasn't much bigger'n you are now. We all had one, but I made her this one special out of calico. Didn't do much good, though—your mother couldn't stand to pick cotton. That was one thing I couldn't much stand myself. It was just so hard an' it was a push. Oh, you'd get up way early an' go to the field. 'Cept for dinner, you'd stay there 'til night. Oh, it was hard."

A sudden sparkle in her eyes and a flush of laughter brought the little girl to rapt attention. "I'll never forget the time your mama tried to get out of pickin' cotton. She cooked her up a real nice scheme, yessir, and it worked—for awhile. The only way anybody ever got out of pickin' cotton was if they was sick. Well, your mama decided if that's what it took, that's what she'd do. An' she knowed she couldn't just say, 'I'm sick'—she had to *be* sick.

"Well, they'd all been out in that field only 'bout an hour or two, an' they all of a sudden heard all this coughin' and carryin' on. An' they looked to where it was comin' from, an' there wuz Ida over there jest a-throwin' up all over the place. Grandpa went an' picked her up an' brung her to the house, an' she stayed there restin' all day.

"This happened a coupla times. Grandpa got suspicious 'cause she didn't have no fever, an' by nightfall she'd be chipper an' lively as could be. So, he decided that nex' time he'd find out what was what. He begun to stay purty even with the row she was workin' so he could watch her outta the corner of his eye.

"Well, sure enough, it happened again—only this time, he saw how she was doin' it. She was stickin' her finger down her throat to make herself throw up! Grandpa didn't say a word about what he saw. He just picked her up as usual an' headed for the house. He later said he was havin' an awful hard time keepin' a straight face about it.

"When they got to the house, he brought her into the kitchen and said, 'Mama, this poor chile is sick again.' He was winkin' at me while he talked. 'I'm getting real worried about Ida. Don't you think it's time we gave her some medicine? She might die on us if we don't.'

"I says, 'Yes, I think we ought to. I just boiled some fresh remedy last week,' an' I started for the cupboard.

"Well, Lord have mercy, your mama went to confessin' right fast about how she wasn't sick an' how she'd rather have a whippin' than take that medicine! Grandpa was tryin' real hard not to bust out laughin'.

"Anyways, she didn't get any medicine or a whippin'. Grandpa took her back with him to finish pickin' cotton. He said he reckoned that was the worst punishment she could get anyhow.

"Pickin' cotton really was backbreakin'—out in that boilin' sun, bent over all day. Why, if I pass a cotton patch to this day, I turn my head. You'd get a bagful, then you'd have to go somewhere to empty it on a sheet. If I picked two hundred pounds a day, I done very well. Old Miz Thompson out here could just go down that row an' first thing you know, she had three hundred or over.

"I'd rather pull corn, pull fodder—anything! An' I guess pickin' peas'd come after that—those dried hulls'd poke through the sack an' stick an' cut you.

"But there was one good thing about it. When Grandpa'd sell his first bale of cotton, he'd always get a hoop of cheese. And, my, we did enjoy that!"

They left the crib together to continue their treasure hunt—the little girl proudly wearing her mother's cotton sack and carrying her grandma's egg basket.

Nona

The weathered five-gallon bucket utters shrill squeaks as it jump-swings on its rusted handle. A chipped-tooth hoe is strapshot across strong, bent shoulders. Worn shoes lay flapping tracks in inch-thick powdered dust along the field road. A garden waits tending along the hill.

Nona is a large woman and quick to tell you, "Old Miz Moore always told me I had the biggest hands and feet she ever saw."

She lifts her seventy-four years easily over the knee-high fence that holds in the garden. Soon, the rhythmical chop, chop of her rusty hoe will be all that stirs the blanket weight of the still, hot summer air.

"I used to have a garden the year-round here.
We'd have cabbage all winter, nearabouts.
An' turnips an' lots of things.
We eat good on the farm.
Never did go without.

"I still sell peanuts and lima beans
    to the stores in town.
One of the presidents of the biggest banks around
    drives all the way out here
to buy my lima beans.

"I just love to farm all the way around.
I don't care nothin' much about the house.
I'd rather be out.
And I'd just rather see a garden grow
    as to eat it near.

“But the farm ain’t nothin’ but a gamble,
’cause you don’t know
what you’ll make.
You can sow the seed,
but then you just have to trust
in the Lord
to do somethin’.”

Marge

Ain't no two girls nowhere worked as hard as me and my sister, Lizzie, worked. But the summer our oldest brother, Frank, came home from his first year in college, Lizzie 'bout got a little too smart for both of us.

One day that summer, Lizzie and me had to take guano in the distributor to work the field. They wanted us to use this old bull that hadn't never been true broke in to pull the distributor. So, we went to the barn and got him hitched up. We was right skittish about using him, but when I tapped him, he started right off. Then we begun to think he might work purty good.

Well, I reckon we got as far as from here to the big pecan tree down yonder, and down he went. He sulled on us. And he just lay there. We pushed, and we pulled, and we did everything we could think of to get him up. He wouldn't get up or move for Jesus. Just kept on laying there.

Well, Lizzie set her jaw, reached into her apron pocket, and says, "This'll move him!" and pulled out a box of matches.

I says, "What are you gonna do?"

She says, "We're gonna set his tail on fire."

Well, we did it. We struck a match and lit his tail afire. We lit the bush on his tail and stuck it right up his rump. And you know what? He lay there! That beat anything I ever seen. That rascal lay there and his rump burned. That bull lay there! He never moved.

There that distributor was, full of guano, and us a-trying to get that bull up, when Ma rang the bell for us to come to dinner.

I said, "Lord, Lizzie, there's the dinner bell. We can't leave him here."

She says, "We'll unhitch him from the distributor and go to the house." Says, "We'll let the son-of-a-gun lie here!"

And then when we got away from him about as far as that big tree down yonder, he raised his head up high. I said, "Lizzie, he's gonna get up. He'll beat us to the house." Sure enough, before we got to the little holler, he'd passed us running to the house. I said, "There he goes!"

Lizzie says, "I could kill him! I could kill him! Ain't that somethin'!"

He just went LOPIN' up the hill.

I says, "Well, Lord have mercy, when we ever gonna get the gears off him?"

"I hope he'll die with 'em on!" Lizzie hollered.

The boys at the house just died laughin' at us. I declare, they laughed—especially Frank.

When my daddy come up and seen that switch burnt off his tail, he said, "Who set the bull afire?"

Lizzie said, "I done it, Papa. He wouldn't pull the distributor and fell down over in the field, and I set his switch afire."

Papa just laughed.

Lizzie and me never did hitch that bull up n'more. The boys did. They tried to break him in to work right. They'd get him on the road, and he'd plow the road all to pieces. But you walk out in the field and stick the plow down, and he'd lay down ever' time. He'd fall right down. That was the orneriest animal I ever did see!

Cousin Sue Bea, on How to Succeed

Farmin's somethin' you got to do
when it's time to do it.
If you don't do it
when the time's right
You'll lose it.
There ain't no tearin' out
an' no hangin' back.

Mag Pickens

There they all were. Caught in one split second to tell forever what they felt—the whole lot of them. Out of carefully dusted dime store frames came the frowns, the bashful grins, the formal stances feigned to impress, the wistful eyes of generations of them. That varnished side table must have held on its doilied top every Pickens in the county. Or so it seemed.

Picking up one of the ovaled groups for a closer look (although every detail had long since been set to memory), Mag admonished, "I think our children are better people for having been raised on a farm. They got a good education around here, 'cause farming teaches you to make your own judgments about things. They learned good horse sense—common sense.

"I had ten children. Had five boys an' five girls. It wuz hard for 'em, but they all grew up healthy. They went to school, and when they come in, they went to work in the field or doin' up the things, an' they worked 'til night.

"Back then, when you had a baby they used t'want you to stay in bed ten days . . . at least . . . after the baby was born. Wouldn't even let you up to use the pot. But I never did do that. I had to git back to the field an' take my babies with me. I carried them babies t' the field an' put 'em in the best shade I could find, is how they was treated. An' I'd usually have a baby crib or somethin' t'put the little baby in, an' the others played out on the ground.

"As soon as they was old enough to work, they went t'work. I've seen that little Lee when the plow handles'd knock him down, an' he'd jest jump up an' go again. I think about my oldest un', Tom. Now, I study about him. He was six years old when Uncle Bill made him a little plow. He'd plow from mornin' 'til night—following the mule.

"An' my girls worked as hard as the boys did. 'Law me, yes! They'd cut wheat with those old scythe cradles, you know, and they'd bind the wheat—I did that, up 'til they got big enough. And so they'd go right behind that and tie the wheat in bundles. It was to shock and then carry to the house an' git ready for a thrashin'.

"It was hard work, yes, but we was all raised that way. An' lots of times it was even fun, 'cause we all worked together, an' we'd try to make a game out of almost every job we had to do. Some folks didn't work that way, but it sure gave us a lot more pleasure. It gave us all a good sense of humor.

"After work at night, the family'd rest and enjoy each other. We'd parch corn, pop popcorn, bake potatoes in the fire . . . in the wintertime, we'd all enjoy locust beer and persimmon beer.

"Families were closer because we didn't have television, an' we didn't have lotsa things that we have now. Children'd mind you more. There were with you more—all the time. Now children don't seem to be with their parents much.

"Just the other Sunday, we made a picture of the fifth generation here. I have about eighty great-grandchildren and one great-great-grandchild. I'm 'bout the oldest one around these parts."

Folding her arms across her apron, Mag stepped back and cocked her head to once more proudly survey her people—her family of the earth.

Bertha, on the Music of Work

Mama had a little room
    out there
    in the cotton house.
In the winter she'd go
    out there
and make her own cloth
    on the loom.

The cloth she wove was brown.
    She cut Tom and Will britches
    out of that cloth she made.
That's what they wore to school.

She'd set and pedal that loom,
    and it was goin' up and down—
    jus' like an organ pedal—
    out there
    in the cotton house.

Estelle, on Little Pleasures

Mama'd save up eggs
and buy her thread at the store
with them eggs.
Sometimes
she'd buy a little snuff, too.

Comfort, on Self-Sufficiency and Store-bought Treats

We gen'rlly bought
        sugar, coffee, salt, and sometimes flour
at the store.
Rest of it
        we made or growed
ourselves.
When we got on up,
        we'd buy
a box of soda crackers.
Now, that was a treat!

Advertised Specials—1910 Union County, NC

LADIES' SHOES

Special lot Fine Shoes, $2.00. Quality made in latest styles. Removal Sale Price...............$1.27

Ladies Finer Vici Kid Shoes, Fancy $2.50. Sale Price..$1.53

Ladies finest Patent Kid $4.00. Shoe Removal Sale...$2.87

All Children's Shoes are Special Removal Sale Priced.

LADIES' UNDERWEAR

Heavy fleeced Pants and Vests, worth 35 cents each. Removal Sale Price.................10 cents

DRESS GOODS

A choice lot of Dress Goods, worth 50 cents per yard. Special Sale Price..................19 cents

Dress Goods worth up to 75 cents per yard. Removal Sale Price..............................33 cents

DRY GOODS

Unbleached Domestic worth 8 cents. Removal Sale Price.. 6 1/2 cents

Calico—American and Simpson. Removal Sale Price..5 cents

Outing Cloth worth 10 cents. Removal Sale Price..6 cents

Outing Cloth worth 15 cents, Removal sale price..7 1/2 cents

Fancy New Gingharis in latest Spring patterns. Removal Sale Price................................5 cents

GROCERIES

19 lbs. Best Granulated Sugar. Removal Sale Price..$1.00

2 lbs. good Roasted Coffee. Removal Sale Price...28 cents

2 lbs. Pea Perry Coffee. Removal Sale Price...35 cents

3 Cans Apples, Corn or Pears...............24 cents

3 Packages Grandmas Washing Powder. Removal Sale Price..............................10 cents

Best Tar Soap. Removal Sale Price 4 cents

10 cent size plug of Tobacco. Removal Sale Price...5 cents

DRUGS AND TOILET ARTICLES

Syrup of Figs, 50 cent bottle. Removal Sale Price...10 cents

Whycoff's Cough Syrup. Removal Price ....19 cents

Red Rose Pomade, worth 15 cents. Removal Sale Price...9 cents

Mentholatum Salve, Removal Sale Price ....19 cents

25 cent Size Bottle of Water-Proof Shoe Polish. Removal Sale Price...............................11 cents

(Items contained in 1910 editions of Monroe Enquirer.*)*

Sadie, on the Payoffs of Planning

We had a big fireplace
    in our kitchen.
And Ma and Pa'd give us
a week apiece
    to make the fires.

I had a week,
    John, Charles, Susie, Lottie—
    all of us,
had a week to get up
    and make the mornin' fire.

So when my week came
    in the wintertime,
why, I'd look out ahead
    for my splinters and pine knots.
And boy, I'd get in that kitchen,
and I'd have a big, roaring fire
    in a little bit.

Mary Elizabeth, on the Household Thermometer

Ice'd be standing
    in the milk
    in the kitchen
on cold winter mornings.

Maisie, on How the Guilford Sisters Stayed Warm at Night

Our house was two-story.
There was one big room upstairs.
It had never been divided into rooms.
        I don't know why.
Us girls slept up there.
It wasn't heated.
Just the kitchen was heated
and the room where you'd sit
at night.

We had sheepskins
we'd warm before the fire
        and run and put on the beds.
We'd jump right in
an' it felt purty good
        under all that cover.

Melva, on How Independence is the Way You Earn It

Fourth of July was our big day!
Papa gave us a field of cotton to hoe
        ahead of time.
He said, "If you finish that field,
        I'll let you go to the Fourth of July.
        If you don't finish, you don't go—
        you stay here and hoe cotton."
Talk about diggin'!
We three
dug our heads off
to get to go to town
on our horse, Lily Belle.

Lord, they'd have parades
and greasy poles
an' all such as that.

We didn't ever miss
a Fourth of July
in town.

Fiddles Racing
Feet Tapping
Bodies Twirling
"Buggies Coming!"
Kids Chasing
Laughter Ringing
Hands Clapping
Tables Sagging
"Cider Chilling!"
Secrets Sliding
Kisses Flying

Chloe, on Having a Time after Layin' By

"It's strange to me that with all the push-button convenience in their homes today, people don't have time to visit like they used to. We used to go an' spend the DAY with people when we'd get through layin' by, you know.

"Why, I've square danced many a time in neighbors' homes. Our daddy was the best fiddler there was. Yes, he never had a lesson in his life, but he could play anything on earth! He could sit there and just fiddle—oh, it was a sight in this world!

"And we used to have some good singin's and candy-pullings. And then we'd get together for corn shuckings and cook up everything we could find. Why, the women'd cook for a week. And I wonder now how we managed when we had no refrigeration. I can see pies and cakes on every bed and dresser we had in the place. Cook whole sheep, whole cows—and how many chickens!

"What a time we did have!"

Miz Fincher Recounts How Life Started Some Lessons for her the Year Cousin Jim Finished School

Ma'd have housecleaning in March.
That was our biggest cleaning of the year.
We'd take all the furniture out in the yard,
then scald and scour every room.
After we were done with that,
we'd clean the furniture
and carry it all back inside.

The year cousin Jim finished school
me and Ma did that,
then went to New Bethel school breakin'
in a two-horse wagon that night.
I was tired to death.
Ma was tired, too,
but she says, "Aunt Lou Starnes wants us to go."

So, we hitched the wagon
and put straw on the floor.
Then we set two or three old chairs in there
an' we went up to Aunt Lou's in that wagon
and got them
and went to the school breakin'.

School breakin'
was when school closed for the year.
They'd have dialogues and speeches.
We'd take sheets from home
and run them around on a wire for the curtain.

We had the biggest time that night.
I'll never forget that.
Cousin Jim did good when he gave his speech
        about democracy.
Aunt Lou said he'd practiced for a week.

Cousin Jim was killed
        just a few months later
        overseas
        in what they said would be the war
                to end them all.
                'Twern't so.
I never saw things quite the same again.

Second Cousin Lucy, on Giving the Men a Break

Me or my chil'ren
used to take water
          out to the fields
for the men
          where they was plowin'.

Women didn't gen'rlly
          do the plowin'
unless it had to be done,
an' there wasn't no men
          around to do it.

But in the afternoon
we'd take the men
water
and somethin' for them to eat —
          bread an' onions
          an' things like that.

Sometimes
we'd take 'em
        a bit of 'lasses cake.
We made the best
        homemade molasses
I've *ever* tasted.
And those cakes
        were real good.
I've seen our daddy
turn the plowstock over
        and sit down on that
        and eat his snack.
Their shirts were so wet
you could see the salt.

’Lasses Cakes

½ cup butter
½ cup sugar
½ cup molasses
2 eggs
½ cup hot, strong coffee
2 cups flour
¼ tsp. salt
1 tsp. soda
1 tsp. cinnamon

Melt the butter in the hot coffee. In a separate bowl, beat the eggs, then add the sugar and molasses to them, mixing well. Sift the dry ingredients together. Slowly add your butter-hot coffee mixture to the eggs, stirring well. Add your sifted ingredients a little at a time. Drop the soft batter a teaspoonful at a time onto a greased tin. Bake about ten minutes at 350°. (This can also be done by pouring the batter into a buttered, floured tin and baking for 20 minutes at 350°. Cool and cut into squares.)

Make a frosting by combining 4 tbsp. milk with one cup of confectioner’s sugar and adding vanilla to taste. Pour frosting on while ’lasses cakes are hot.

Fronia, on Looking to Each Other

We thought we was having a hard time,
but it was the best time of our lives.
        Yes, siree!
We had to make our own good times.
There wasn't nothing else but each other
        to look to
to have a good time.
We visited and spent time with each other.
Kids'd spend a week at a time
        at cousins' houses
an' have the best time—
        Lord have mercy!

Willabele Muses while Unboxing her New Easter Dress

We'd all go to town
        about once a year.
That was a big thrill.

Our family usually went
        early on in the spring
'cause all the women
        had to have
a new spring hat for church.

We went in the wagon—
that was the only way we had
        to travel.
Went to church in a wagon.
Prosperous folks went in buggies.

Women don't wear hats
                                much anymore.
But I still go to town
every year
        about Easter.

Stora and Et

"Stora, do you remember when the last one was?"

"Not rightly, but I think . . . let me see. . . . Yes, it was the year Howard had his heart attack. We never had another one after that."

"I don't think anybody has them anymore. I haven't heard of one in years."

The two sisters were walking gingerly along the green mowed bank of their small pond, which lay halfway across the pasture behind the old barn. Et and Stora occasionally enjoyed early morning summer strolls around the pond before the sun got too high and the mosquitoes too pesky. Stora was getting a little assist from her bare wood cane, an implement Et disdained for her own use. The two had set up housekeeping together at the home place after Stora's husband, Howard, had died. Et had never married, but family lore had it that it wasn't for lack of beaus. Seems Et was much in love with a young man, but something happened—nobody will say what—and he left these parts—nobody will say why.

Stora stopped, leaned on her cane, and looked wistfully out over the opaque waters. "I can just see all those men out in that pond with that big net, seining up all those fish."

"Humph!" Et chimed in. "I can just HEAR all those men out there whooping it up to high heaven, having the time of their lives. Why, when we had a pond seining, there were cousins and neighbors from all around here. Sometimes there were too many to get in the pond, so some had to just follow along the bank and watch."

Pointing with her cane, Stora said, "They'd take off their shoes and wade in wearing their overalls or jeans. They'd start at the shallow end down there and slowly move the length of the pond to the dam end, pushing that big net ahead of them. They'd have a mess of jumping, flopping bass, brim, catfish, and some odd pieces of tree limb by the time they got to the dam end and hauled it all out."

Et chuckled, remembering how much fun the men had teasing each other, and how much laughter had echoed from that old pond. "Remember, Stora, when Aaron just turned his section of the pond into a storm of white-water, swearing that a cooter was having his toe for dinner? And I can just see them the time all the men grabbed George and threw him back into the pond after it was all over as payback for all the ribbing he had done to the rest of them all day." Both sisters laughed heartily.

"Yes, we women always watched and enjoyed it all from the banks," grinned Stora. "Then, we'd leave the men to clean all those fish while we went back to the house to fix the rest of the food. There'd be long tables created from planks laid across sawhorses and covered with tablecloths. We women would troop in and out of the house carrying bowls of cole slaw and potato salad, jars of homemade pickles, gallons of iced tea, tins and tins of pies, plates of sliced tomatoes and cucumbers, and plates of raw, sliced potatoes. We just kept that screen door slamming, just singing a song on its hinges."

"And don't forget the loaves of white bread," chimed Et. "We couldn't get along without our fry bread."

"Once we set the food on those long tables, we covered it all with sheets to protect everything from flies and those yellow jackets and bees."

Stora continued, "Some of the women were busy getting the pots ready to fry all those fish the men would soon be bringing up from the pond. We had three large, black wash pots at the last seining. Wood fires were lit under each pot, and we brought extra firewood to lay nearby for ready use. We filled each pot halfway up with lard for the frying. We had a table near the pots where we kept dishpans full of meal to roll the fish in, then toss them in the pots to fry."

"Don't forget the fry bread," Et chimed in again. "It was the last thing to be fixed. It was done after all the fish had finished frying, and the grease in the pots had a lot of fried meal bits in it from the fish. We'd dump whole loaves of sliced white bread into the pots and they'd fry a crispy brown. We didn't have hushpuppies like you have now. I've had hushpuppies many a time, but I must say, I like fry bread better." She paused. "Maybe that's because I can't get it anymore."

"While all this was going on," Et continued, "the men were changing into dry clothes and gathering around in chairs. They told a bunch of stories—many of them quite embellished—on each other from their day's adventure. The laughter and chatter just filled the air." Et and Stora wore wide smiles.

Store finished by saying, "When the food was ready, everyone stopped where they were as the most senior man, or the man of best reputation, was asked to give thanks. We all bowed our heads. Then we filled our plates and enjoyed the rest of the afternoon. The first lightning bug was usually the signal it was time to go home."

Et said, "Stora, I think it's time we were getting back, too. This July sun is beginning to get a little warm."

"All right," Stora responded, "but let's stroll all the way around the pond as we go back."

They started off with arms linked together. Stora's voice drifted back through the soft, warm breeze. "Do you remember. . . ?"

Phoebe, on Church and Teacakes

"Bout ever'body went to church around here,
tho' some folks'd as like to go t'the creek
        as go t'church.

We'd usually knock off about noon on Saturday,
and the girls'd start rolling their hair for Sunday.
We used to plait it and braid it
        to make it curly.

Sometimes there'd be two sermons a day on Sunday
        and dinner on the grounds.
We didn't have tables.
We just spread a tablecloth on the ground.

Mama used to take teacakes in her pocketbook
        to church for us children—
to settle us down when we got wigglesome.
An' I'd always wiggle
so she'd open her pocketbook
and give me a teacake.

Phoebe's Teacake Recipe

2 cups flour
2 tbsp. sugar
1 tsp. salt
4 tsp. baking powder
3 tbsp. butter
1 egg, beaten well
½ c. milk

Sift the dry ingredients together twice. Cut the dry ingredients into the butter until small pebble size. Add the milk to the beaten egg, mix; add slowly to the dough, mixing well. Knead a few times on a floured board, roll out and cut into squares. Put in a buttered pan and brush with melted butter. (You can then sprinkle with sugar, if you wish.)

Bake at 400° for 15 minutes.

Aunt Rowena Laments the Effect of Air-conditioning on Sunday Afternoon Sociability, when Visiting was Done Outdoors and it was Considered Unforgivably Rude not to Wave and Speak to Passersby

You don't
never see
nobody
a-sittin' around
under a shade tree
no more.

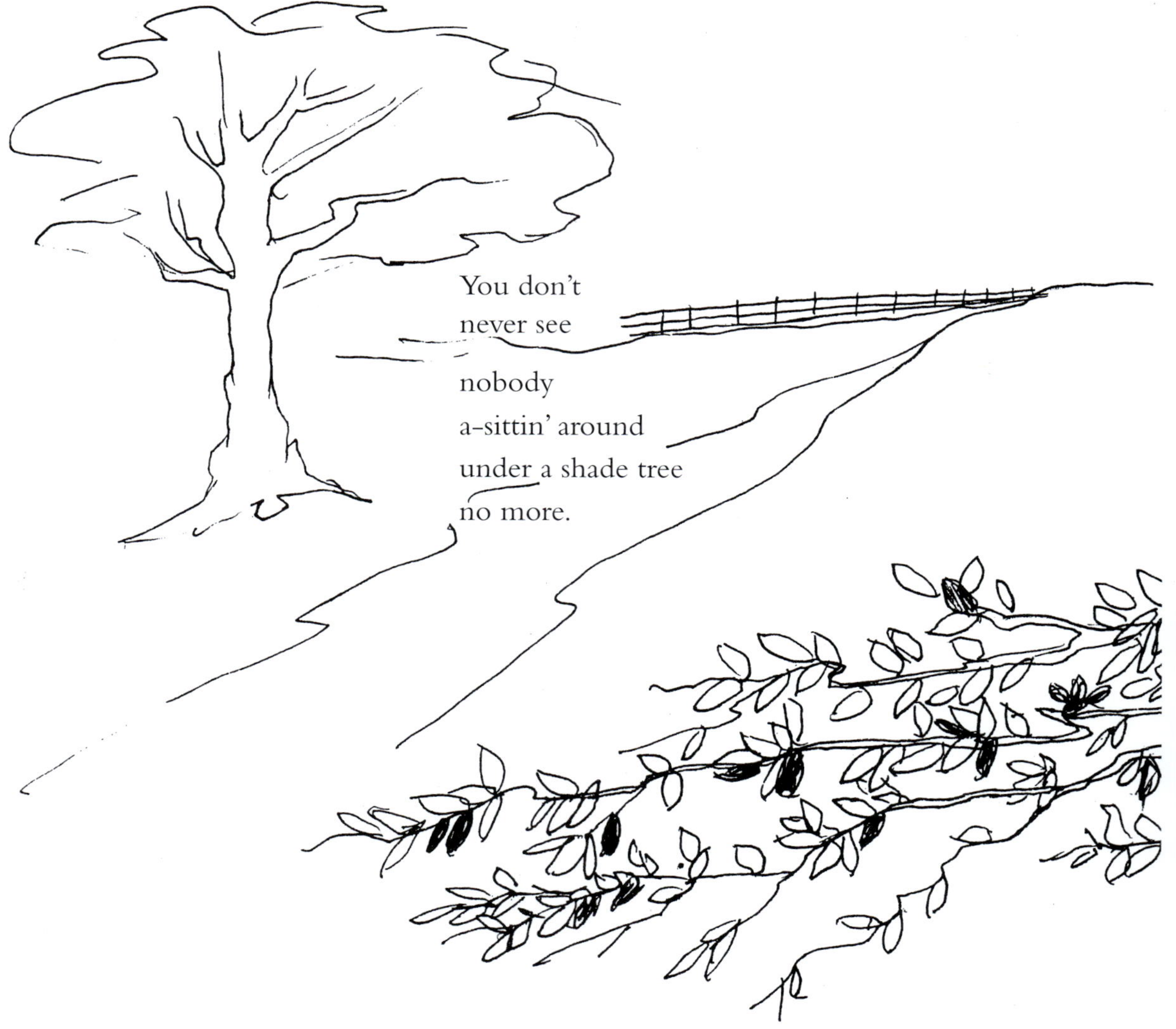

Ruth

"I don't know. I jest don't know," she mumbled as she picked up a last, fat acorn to add to her already full apron. She sighed as she sat down in a rickety chair shadowed by a majestic old oak, and began sorting the acorns for the harvest wreath she made every year.

"This old tree we're a-settin' under, it's older'n you—older'n me—older'n Time itself, I sometimes think. Don't reckon nobody knows how long it's been here. But it ain't gonna be much longer." The tree answered with a dry rustle, sending down a shower of brown and gold leaves—each leaf as big as two hand spreads.

"That tree and I been here together as long as I can remember," she said, looking up into the towering limbs that spread through the sky like meandering country roads. The sun, snagged by a twig far above, sparkled in light spills down through the branches and played in her eyes, making her squint at her old friend.

"I played under this tree as a child an' it'uz full growed, even then. My daddy used to shoe horses under this tree. See that peg 'bout head high in the trunk? He put that there to hang his shirt on. Always did love the shade this tree gave.

"My husband Sam—God rest his soul—proposed to me on this very spot. We'uz married here. Preacher didn't much like marryin' out o' church, but we didn't care. An' my babies, they all grew up playin' under this tree. Oh, we had good times! We'd have dinner out here in the summer lots of days. And when company came on Sundays, we'd all sit out here near all day long, visitin'. Why, this tree is like family."

A touch of despair she wanted to conceal crept into her voice and crowded the mellow look of memory from her face. "I don't know. I jes' don't know. My family's all dead now—my husband and my babies. I'm all that's left. Ain't got no sisters or brothers. An' this tree's all I got. It's the only livin' thing I have left in this world. An' they're comin' to cut it down next week. They're wantin' to widen the road an' straighten out the curve in front of the house here so it can carry more of them cars, they say.

"I've asked 'em couldn't they widen the road on the other side along the field there, an' please leave this tree standin'. But they say no. They say the state's done laid the plans and got a right to do what they want.

"I jes' don't know if I can stand it. When they cut down this tree, ever'thing I got to cling to will be gone. Seems like I just can't bear to think of it. An' I know I can't stand to watch 'em cut it down. I don't know where I'll go, but I just can't be here when they do it."

Looking with wet eyes at the acorns in her lap, she said, "I don't know . . . I jes' don't know."

Mary Rebecca, on Neighborliness

Before telephones,
        before automobiles,
neighbors depended more on each other.
If anybody in the community was sick,
the neighbors'd go in
        and plant their crops
        and even harvest the crops.

Miss Minnie Cogitates

Hope m'die,
somedays I get to
 settin' here an' studyin'
 'bout way back yonder,
an' I cain't believe it.
I cain't hardly believe
 that times was back then
 like they was.

To think what we're livin' in now
 an' how it was back then.
An' I just got to say that
 back then was better.
It was harder, it was.

Now they got automobiles
an' they ain't satisfied here
 'til they get yonder,
an' they ain't satisfied there
 an' go on som'ers else.
That's the way people is now.
 They just in a whirl and a twirl.
Can't be satisfied nowhere.

Reesa, on how There Didn't Used to be So Many of Us

You'd go
for miles and miles
drivin' an old horse and buggy
before you'd come to a house.

Sister Ro' Reveals How Some Folks Got More Money for Picking Cotton than Others Did

Leonard
put rocks
in his cotton sheet
to make it
weigh heavier.

Velda, on Cotton Colds

Cotton is the hardest thing ye'll ever have to work with! We'd all pick cotton in the fields. We'd pull the cotton bolls off, and then pick it by the fire at night. Me and my sister Flonnie have pulled off bolls with ice in them, and piled it up on the front porch—that big-old front porch up there.

At night, we'd have to sit up and pick out the cotton—that cold cotton. We'd put potatoes in the fire and roast them. We'd eat 'taters and pick cotton—eat 'taters and pick cotton. Lord, have mercy! And if we had peanuts, we'd parch peanuts.

And set there at night with them old, wet burrs, and they'd give ye a cold. They'd do it! And Pa says don't burn a one—says that's what'll give ya a cold, burnin' them burrs. Says don't pitch them in the fire, just keep them raked back. We didn't dare throw one in the fire. Didn't never catch a cotton cold, neither.

Flonnie and me was pretty lucky about being well and healthy. When we did have somebody sick around here, we'd doctor them with the herbs we'd plant and grow around the garden. I'll lay stake that many of them same herbs is used in medicines today. If nobody didn't go to the doctor anymore'n I do, the doctors'd have t'get them another job.

Miz Hawkins Speculates on Waste and Values

I don't know why in the world—
people used to have rows.
Farm folks now
have rows wide enough
to run a wagon through near 'bout
    in the corn.
I never could understand it!

Sara, on Generosity

I've raised lots of chickens.
I'd raise 'em up
        and then, of course,
there'd be more than I could use.
I've carried chickens in my hand
        —six and eight, now—
and walked to Cross Hill carryin' 'em.

An' I was goin' up a long hill one mornin'.
It was hot, my gracious!
An' one died—smothered to death.
So I carried it up to that big house
and I says,
        "Ain't nothin' wrong with this chicken."
I says, "It just smothered t'death.
        I had a bunch of 'em."
An' I says,
        "You can have it ef you want to."

Arlene, on Starting the Day

Well, you cooked breakfast
just as quick
as you could cook it
an' get to th' field.

Creola's Cornmeal Mush

Add enough cold water to one cup of cornmeal to make a paste. Stir this paste slowly into two quarts of boiling water. Mix it well and add one teaspoon of salt. Cook it, stirring occasionally, for about ten to fifteen minutes. Serve it hot with sugar and milk to taste.

If you want fried mush, take the hot, cooked mush and spread it out in a well-greased baking pan. Let it stand until it gets cold. It will be solid. Cut it into strips about a half-inch wide. Roll these strips in flour and fry them in butter until they're brown. Syrup poured over the fried mush with sausage on the side is the best way to eat it.

Hoe Cakes

Add some salt to taste to cornmeal. Pour scalded milk in it just to moisten, then mix and let it stand for about an hour. Have a hot, greased griddle ready. Pour ⅛ cup of the cornmeal mixture onto the griddle for each hoe cake and smooth it out to about ½ inch thick. Brown on both sides. Serve hot with syrup or molasses for breakfast.

Agnes, on Learning to Do With

During the Depression,
we had to mix cornmeal
with our biscuit flour
to make it last longer.

Prices on the farms
went down so,
you couldn't get
anything
for nothin'
you grew.

Nelly, Pulling a Pan of Biscuits from her Electric Range, Remembers her Advent into the Modern World

Woodstoves was all we had
        back then.
An' you just didn't cook too much
        to have it wasted up.
I had me a wood burnin' stove
        'til John got his right arm
                tore off
an' I couldn't get n'more wood
                fer it.
I never could chop wood m'self,
        but I've helped 'em split it.

Auberta says Good Families Have Good Stories, and This is Hers

My daddy had one of the first cars around here. Oh, it was a real purty model. But I never did learn to drive. To tell you the truth, he never did either. He had the car brought out here an' kept it parked in the barn where the best wagon was. The first day it was here, he and Mama and all the rest of us went out there to see about takin' a ride in it. Papa said he wanted to try it first to see if it'uz alright.

He got it turned on—we wuz all kinda nervous—an' got in it. He made it outta the barn an' all over the yard just fine. Then he headed back to the barn, an' we all thought he was gonna stop so we could get on. But he went straight through that barn an' come out the other side, hollerin', "Whoa! Whoa!"

Mama started yellin', "What's the matter, James? Stop that thing!"

By this time, he was around the other side of the barn comin' through again, still hollerin', "Whoa! Whoa!" Mama was jumpin' up an' down, an' we was all yellin'.

Seems like the fellers that sold Papa the car had told him all about how to get it started, but they'd forgot to tell him how to stop it. Well, he rode that thing 'til it run outta gas. Then he and the boys pushed it into the barn. Papa never drove that car again. The boys learned to drive it, but Papa'd just snort ever' time they passed by him in it.

That little happenin' has turned into a family story that I reckon will be passed along down the line. Papa sure did come in for his share of ribbin' from it. He died about a year after he got that car. I don't think the two was related.

Earlene, Recalling the Perils of Progress

Dr. Pete was the first one
        ever had a car around here.
An old field hand lived
        across the branch there
an' he hadn't hardly ever
        been off the place.
An' he seen Dr. Pete
        go up the road in that car.
He uz scared t'death.
He went runnin' t'the house.
He left the mule 'n ever'thing.
An' he tole his wife—
"Lawd, God, Miriam!
Yonder g-goes the Gospel Train
an'— an' there ain't but
t-two people in it!"

Nan's Pride: The Dinner Bell

"The field hands used to say,
        'If Miss Nan goes off an' gets sick
                an' if she ain't too sick,
        let her ring the bell
        'cause we cain't hear nobody else
                but her.'"

Faith Recalls an Unexpected Guest

Grandpa was settin'
at the head of the table
as usual.
He and the boys
had come in
from the fields
when the dinner bell
was rung.

He had a beard,
a long beard,
like most men had
back then.
None of his children
had ever seen his face.

I was lookin'
at a piece of straw
caught midways down
in his beard.
Suddenly,
his beard began to move.

I thought
maybe
it was chewin' movin',
but it wasn't.
Just then
I saw a little green head
poke out
and a long, green body
begin to follow.

I hollered!
A commotion commenced.
Ever'body
    was doin'
        or sayin'
    something—
except Grandpa.

He just looked down
    at his beard,
grabbed that little snake
    behind its head
and walked out the door.

He was back in a minute,
sat down at the table
    like nothing had happened
and said,
    "Your mama's cookin's
        so good,
    you can't never tell
        who's likely
        to stop by
        for dinner."

Guess you couldn't expect
    nothing less
from a man
who walked barefooted
    and half-starved
all the way home
    from Virginny
    after The War.

Cousin Alice's Approach to Work

I didn't think nothin'
'bout not likin' to do things,
'cause I had to do 'em.
Oh, hit was just work -
ever'where you turned!
But I reckon I enjoyed it.
I worked, anyway,
whether I enjoyed it
or not.

Rebecca Jane, on Sewing for Sowing, among Other Things

We sewed up our own bedsheets.
Never did buy any ready-made.
The sheeting was five cents a yard.

We made our bloomers, too.
They was made out o' black sateen.
I sure didn't bundle up
        in a lot of underwear
in hot weather.
        No, sirree!

We women did most of our sewing
        in the wintertime.
Sewed up
        quilts and
what we was gonna wear
                in the fields
        come spring sowing.

Inez, on Winding up the Week at the Sutton Place on Richardson Creek

On Saturdays
we'd be a-bakin'
an' scourin' floors
        with an ole shuck broom.
Put sand on the floor
        an' take an ole shuck broom
        an' scour it
an' then rinse that off.
We didn't have rugs back then—
        didn't know what rugs was.
No kind.
We didn't know what linoleum was.
We had wood floors.

Old Miz Griffin, on the Tried and True

Old tractors!
I despise 'em!
I'd rather have a mule
any day!

Lily Mae Allows as How Wash Days was Full Days

We didn't wash clothes in a sink—
        wasn't no such thing as a sink.
We had an old, wooden tub
        with a big board
an' we rubbed our clothes on the board
        with our own homemade soap.

Then we boiled them.
Put 'em in a washpot
        an' put fire around it
        an' water in it
an' boiled the clothes.
That helped get the dirt out.

When our well went dry,
I had to take our clothes
        to the branch
        and wash them.
        Hung them on bushes
        to dry.
Done that many a time.

Verla

Me milk cows? Why, I grew up milking cows. Had to go across that old orchard down there to get to the barn. That's why I'll never forget the year the big snow came. That was three years before I got married. Rance Plyler was staying at our house that year, and there come a big snow and sleet on top of it. Rain, you know, and then sleet, and it froze on top of that snow. And we had to go to the cow barn that morning and milk. I think there was five cows we was milking.

Well, Rance got up, got his clothes on, and we eat breakfast. It was early. You always had to milk early. While we was all eating our bread and gravy, Ma says, "Well, we got t'git to the barn some way or n'other to milk."

Rance says, "Well, I'll go down there, Miz Grace, and milk the cows." Says, "I'll go and you all stay here."

And Ma says, "No, we'll not put all that on you now."

And I says, "Well, I'll get ready and go with you."

So me and Rance started. An' we got out there to the orchard where the path to the barn started. I tell you now, that path looked *slick*.

And Rance says, "Verla, wait a minute." He says, "Let me get a mattock and I'll dig holes. I'll go in front of you and dig a hole, and you can sock your heel in it, and you won't slip down."

Well, I stood there shiverin' and shakin' while he went back to the cotton house. He got that old mattock, and here he come. And he'd dig a hole over this way, and then he'd dig a hole over that way—just about a step, y'know. And we got to the cow barn, at last. I was plumb stiff with cold by the time we got through milkin'. It was so cold, the milk would steam when it hit them icy buckets. We finally got them cows milked and had about three buckets of it.

When we was ready to start back, I said, "Leave the old mattock here. We'll git it sometime today."

"No," Rance said, "I'm gonna take it. We ain't comin' back down here 'til this evenin'. You take two of them buckets. I'll carry t'other one and the mattock."

I was in front of him, goin' on up with the milk. We got about halfway up there, and my foot slipped. I pitched backwards, slammed into Rance, and we both tumbled down onto that ice and slid near halfway back to the barn. Spilled ever durned bit of that milk. And we had milked hard. My hands was froze.

I says, "Well, Rance!"

An' he says, "Don't grieve over spilled milk. Git yourself on to the house and let it go to the devil." I can just hear him saying that now.

I went on to the house and Ma says, "What happened?"

I says, "I fell down and knocked Rance down and spilt the milk. Rance tole me to carry it and put it on me and I knowed I'd spill it."

Ma says, "Oh, my! That was what we was gonna drink tonight."

I says, "Well, we can drink water. We can just drink water."

That was the year I first started drinking coffee. And I ain't never put no milk in it. Just a little sugar.

Nettie, on How to Have Fresh Apples in December

We'd wrap apples in paper
    and put them in boxes
        under the bed.
They'd stay crisp and good
    until Christmas.

Muriel, Violet's Youngest, Recalls Christmas Goodies as She Cuts a Piece of Her Own Fresh-made Blackbottom Pie

Lord, Ma'd make cakes for Christmas—
    cover the bed with 'em . . .
Dare us young'uns to pull out a ball o' candy.
"Oh," she said, "don't you pull those green leaves."
She had a little green vine out there in the yard—
    had little green leaves on it,
    had little blue blossoms.
She'd go get them leaves,
    an' clean 'em up right clean,
an' put 'em on the balls o' candy and cakes.
An' beat them eggs!
She'd beat them eggs by hand
    'til it looked like her hand'd come off.
You had to hand-beat egg whites
    to make meringue.
Now folks don't know what hand-beatin' eggs is.

Louise, Finishing a Jaunty Version of "Jolly Old Saint Nicholas" on the Old Upright Piano in Her Parlor

At Christmas,
we didn't give each other gifts
        like we do today—
we didn't have it to give.

Christmas was
        cookin', eatin',
        visitin' and enjoyin'.
That kind of Christmas
        was much better
        than it is today.

Oh, my!
We had so much fun at Christmas!
The children would hang their stockings
        on Christmas Eve for Santa Claus.
An' that orange and apple and raisins
        an' a little bit of candy
you got in your stocking
was something wonderful!

I don't think we ever got any toys.
I do remember
getting a baby doll one time.
It was a nice one,
        packed with sawdust.

Soodie from Prospect, on Ants and Life

These ants bites now,
        I'll tell you the truth!
But I can put up with it.
I've 'bout put up with somethin'
        all m'life!
But . . .
        it's been a pleasure.
There's been a lotta heartache
an' there's
        been a lotta pleasure
                in it.

Zenia Unconsciously Rubs Her Right Arm as She Reflects

I've helped haul
    wheat 'n oats
'til I couldn't
    even reach up
an' put the fork up
        n'more.
About the sorest
    I ever got
    in my life
was bindin'
    wheat 'n oats.

Lorena, on the Joys of Winter Vittles

It'd take two days
to get the potatoes up
and put them in hills
where they wouldn't freeze.

We'd cut up cabbage for kraut.
We'd cut a big 65-gallon barrel
   of cabbage.
Then Ma'd fix it up for kraut.

In the wintertime when it was cold,
we'd sneak in that little shed
and take all that cover off
and eat that kraut.
It'd be just as tender and crisp.

Lord have mercy knows,
we'd eat 'taters and kraut
   all winter.
We'd go out to the smokehouse,
cut a piece of ham meat,
and have ham and gravy
   with them.

Molasses Potatoes

Place three cups cooked, mashed sweet potatoes in a buttered baking dish. Gently boil two tbsp. molasses and one tbsp. butter together for seven minutes, and then pour the mixture over the potatoes. Bake at 325–350° until lightly browned.

Grace, on Courtin'

"That old swing over there puts me in mind of my courtin' days," she said, setting down her okra bucket. "Let's set a spell in it. It's about the coolest place to sit around here this time of day." The rusty chains jerked, and the swing teetered uneasily until Miss Nora's foot pushed firmly against the porch's gap-toothed floor and sent it into an easy, smooth glide.

Wiping the sweat from her forehead with her apron, she said, "Parents back then was real strict about us courtin'. We didn't go out on no such thing as dates then. The boys'd come callin' at the house, an' we'd sit out here or in the parlor an' talk or take walks. There was lots of parties given at folks's homes, an' couples'd court at the parties, too.

"My sister Nell was goin' with this boy, an' she was real smitten with him. Dad didn't have no use for him. Clarence was smart, but he didn't have no parents . . . no raisin'. He uz just jerked up by th' hair o' his head. Dad told Nell he didn't want that boy on the place.

"Since Dad wouldn't allow him around the house, Nell an' Clarence took up correspondin'. Dad never did know about those letters. He uz in the field workin', an' Nell always went to get the mail.

"Anyway, Nell decided to run away an' get married. She an' I slept together, so she told me what she was goin' to do. I uz scared to death, 'cause I knew I'd get a whippin' if Dad found out I knew what she was gonna do, an' I hadn't told him.

"She got up that night about ten-fifteen and went to where she was to meet Clarence down at the highway. I hardly slept.

"Next mornin', I hid the note she'd left on the pillow, an' then I walked out an' said, 'Anybody know where Nell is?'

"Well, that put the ball in the fire.

"Nell and Clarence stayed away from the house for a good time. But afterwhile, Dad came to accept the marriage an' treated the boy just like one of the family. An' I guess nobody can say Nell done wrong, 'cause it was a happy marriage as long as she an' Clarence lived."

Daisy, on What to Say When a Lady Can't Cuss

"Cat's ankle!"
"Red bug's thigh!"

Daisy, on Other Useful Common Expressions

Have enough get-up and get.

Limber as a dishrag.

Sure as green 'simmons set y'teeth on edge.

Raining pitchforks.

Couldn't boil water without scorching it.

A rough row to hoe.

Play 'possum.

Poor as Job's turkey.

Aunt Het, on Maintaining Loveliness

And a lady wouldn't *dare*
        let the sun touch her hands.
Women wore gloves
        to work in outside.
And a bonnet
and sleeves on the arms.
Then,
you had to have
        pretty, un-tanned skin . . .
        creamy and soft.

Hattie

Her body was old and gnarled like the oak trunks in her front yard. Together, they creaked in the wind and bent under the hoarfrost breath of winter. Her clothes blew loosely around her—leaf images shaped by the wind. And each spring the same gingham. Maybe she dressed in starched linens and bright calicos when she was young, but she and her earth had been together too long and were too bound for her to give that much thought to such a superficial art. They each felt the heartbeat, the laughter, the sounds of the other. It counted for them both when the birds nested and the insects flew, when the flowers danced and the corn grew. Lines had run across her cheeks and down her throat in diamond-furrowed patterns like the cracks a hot sun's eternity bakes into the earth. Her arms had grown long over hard years of lifting, hauling, carrying. The hands had toughened to a remarkable strength, but how gently they could lift and tenderly hold the fragile life in newborn things!

And flowers! How Hattie loved flowers. Her luminous, blue-flecked eyes showered image of petunias, hyacinths, pansies, roses, and a rainbow of others that she grew in puddled splashes every year around her sagging, whitewashed house. Hattie was proud that folks came to her to get flowers for weddings, funerals, anniversaries, birthdays—any time celebration or comfort needs came into peoples' lives.

She had a special patch of Baby's Breath out behind the corn crib, and she always cut a little of this to accompany whatever flowers the folks wanted. She said this was her contribution—a little bit of herself—to send along. Some folks paid for the flowers they took in cash, some paid in kind, and some gave nothing. Hattie said the folks who gave nothing for the flowers probably were empty in their pockets or their hearts, and that you couldn't get something from nothing and that maybe the flowers would help fill some of that empty space. She'd tell you with a whispered smile sliding past crinkled crow's feet into her eyes, "Flowers is angels' wings come to earth."

Mindy's Place

Flaming feathery bronze,
gathering gold
        from the low sun,
broomstraw tops tip and weave,
gently brushing her shoulders,
softly brushing away
        the cares, the toils,
sifted over her arms, her back.

Her legs lifting sure
        beneath the dust-tipped skirt,
        the worn, faded apron,
she moves deeper
        into the broomstraw lake
with the swish and swirl
        of long stems
closing the wake
        trailing behind her.

Pausing,
Turning slowly round
        to float
in the coppered peace
of this hidden broomstraw patch
tucked between the sprawling fingers
        of two woods
        reaching for one another.
Her patch.
Her secret place.
Not often visited,
        but always anticipated.

Breathing deeply in the clean, warm air,
the shadow of a smile on her lips,
she bends to her task.
A clutch of broomstraw in one hand,
a strong, low swipe of her dulled knife
            with the other—
soon
there are neat piles
interspersed among the stubble.

She fills her arms
            with the harvested stalks
and carries them
            to the edge of the field
into the flitting shadow-plays
            of a lacy, old cedar.

Drawing a ball of twine
            from her apron pocket,
her nimble fingers begin
to bind the straw into brooms.
A slip-knot over the end,
in-and-out loops
            through the first short way,
then spirals of twine
            the length of the broomspine
to stop
for the long, brushy heads
            left free for sweeping.

Bound tight, knotted well—
she forms her brooms
            with great intent.

Not knee-low or hip-level
as most.
Hers are shoulder-high
with the tall straw
from her secret place.

She binds them and fluffs them,
and smiles again.
She remembers finding this patch
years ago
while looking for blackberries.
She has returned
twice a year since then
and found a purpose in her brooms.

She spends this time
in peace, memory, and hopes,
weaving them all into the brooms
she will wield for her family.

She will sweep cares away,
dust off memories
from the corners,
and keep a clean way
for hopes and dreams
to come and go.

Six brooms finished,
the golden afternoon dimming,
she stands,
wraps the brooms
to nest in her apron,
and sets off for home.

Home,
where she is coming
with the best this woman can bring—
    the tallest, strongest, natural brooms
    in the county,
    ready for the work
    she has for them to do
    from her secret place
    in the corner of the woods
    and the depths of her heart.

Miss Jenny

From a Mockingbird's eye
    on his full-throated rush to the moon,
the earth lies a patchwork below—
    a wing's rustle away
from the hand-stitched quilt on Miss Jenny's bed.

Fields in the textured scraps
    carefully collected and sorted.
Borders and earth pieces threaded together
    with cool, winding creek beds
        trailing red-dust roads,
    with patterned, plowed rows
        waving solids and laces of greens and golds.
    Quilted in farmlands and pieced for repose,
        worked and shaped with strong, knotted hands.
    Tonight she rests peacefully
        in her eighty-ninth year
        under the quilt spread;
    in a while, she will rest
    as well
        in her fine-quilted earth.
    They are the same for Miss Jenny.

Aunt Lucinda Sums It Up

The Good Lord
has been
mighty good
to me.

About the Author

Barbara Funderburk is a native of North Carolina who holds degrees from Wake Forest and East Carolina universities. A former photojournalist, she has worked in television as a writer and producer, in public relations, and has taught English and history in public school. Later, she served as a registered nurse in home healthcare and in training and human resources in hospital settings. Her paintings have been exhibited in galleries and art shows, and are included in several private and corporate collections. Ms. Funderburk lives in Monroe, NC.

About the Book

Count Their Lives in Womanyears was designed and typeset in Bembo by Kachergis Book Design, Pittsboro, North Carolina. *Count Their Lives in Womanyears* was printed by Pacifica Communications of South Korea.